GOD
IS NO
STRANGER

GOD IS NO STRANGER

Translated by Eleanor Turnbull
Photography by Wally Turnbull
Compiled by Sandra L. Burdick

Baker Book House • Grand Rapids, Michigan

Standard Book Number: 8010-0501-9
Copyright © 1970 Baker Book House Company
First Printing, March 1970
Second Printing, December 1971

Preface

Haiti is a land of contrasts; beauty and poverty live side by side. However, one of the greatest contrasts is spiritual, that between the life of a born-again Haitian Christian and the life of a fear-ridden Voodooist. The Christian, freed from guilt and the power of the Evil One, finds love and joy in the person of Christ. His prayers, simple and direct, reflect a genuineness that is both refreshing and heart-warming; sometimes they are sad, and at times even humorous.

In 1968, my husband and I visited the home of Rev. Wallace and Eleanor Turnbull, missionaries in the mountains of Haiti. Eleanor loved to take us to the homes of their beloved mountain people. These Haitian Christians welcomed us into their meager huts and were eager to have prayer with us. As Eleanor translated their prayers, I was overwhelmed by the bond of love God has given to believers. Realizing the uniqueness of their expression, we planned to share them with you. That is how this book happened.

We are grateful to Eleanor for setting aside time in her busy schedule, to translate and record these prayers; to Joyce Garner, mission secretary, who made certain we received copies; to W. Glen Campbell for coordinating our efforts; and Becky Gibson who helped me type and assemble the material.

The lovely pictures were taken by the Turnbulls' eldest son Wally, who is working toward a Master of Fine Arts degree in photography and hopes to work in the field of Christian publications.

I trust that Haitian believers will forgive us for this brief invasion of their spiritual privacy, for we hope that as others read their words, they, too, will find that *God Is No Stranger*.

John 1:12   Sandra L. Burdick

Lord,
We don't get mangos from
   an avocado tree
And we don't get corn
   from the banana plant.
We produce what we are.
Help us to be
   what You need produced.

Lord,
how glad we are
that we don't hold You,
but that You hold us.

Lord,
If we are alive today in spite of
   Hurricanes, hunger, and sickness,
We should say, "Thank You, Lord.
   We must be here for a purpose."

Lord,

Help us not to connect ourselves
   to things.

We may have four dresses today,

But maybe there will be a time
   When we won't have any.

Help us to connect ourselves to
   God's Word.

No one keeps on trying something
   If he never makes progress.
If Satan keeps tempting us,
   It's because we keep giving him
Some encouragement.

Lord,

We have come to Your marketplace.

We know there are plenty of provisions
   in Your market.

We have brought our baskets with us;
   and now we want to go back from
Your market
   with our baskets full of provisions.

The Holy Spirit is our boss,
  We know that He alone
  Remembers the route
  That Jesus walked.
So we know that only He can show
  Us the same way.

Father,
We are all hungry baby birds this morning.
Our heart-mouths are gaping wide,
Waiting for You to fill us.

Jesus, our Brother,

We lie in front of You on our bellies

As we wait for You as a big brother to teach us.

Your words are to us a mirror,

   a bath, a powdering and perfuming.

Then help us to rise up with

   a fresh "toilet"

And go out among the world this week.

All my life I have been just a weed;
  but the other day You pulled me up,
    planted me in Your garden, and
      I became a flower.

I am young and I want to grow
  and be cultivated
    so I can become beautiful.

Lord,
Our skin is black,
    But our sins were blacker.
You have delivered us from sin
And made us white.

Our Great Physician,
Your Word is like alcohol.
When poured on an infected wound,
It burns and stings,
But only then can it kill germs.
If it doesn't burn,
It doesn't do any good.

Lord,
We are like the lady
   Madame Wallace took to the
      Psychiatric Center.
The lady had lost some pages from her book.

We, too, seem to have lost some pages.
   We are unregenerate.
      So we come to You
So You can put us back in the Way.

Lord, I heard a man say,
"I give You my heart."
But this morning I feel
I cannot give only my heart —
I offer my whole self.

Although we lack a dress
   to wear to church,
Lack food at home,
   and have only two cents in our pockets:
The grace of Jesus is enough!

   With this grace,
      we are rich.

Lord,
We are on the edge of the mountain
Which keeps caving in from erosion.
Day by day, more is caved away.

In the world, we are on slippery ground,
Standing on the edge
Of a caving-in mountain.

Speaking about who and what we are
Won't secure us. For safety,
We must step up to higher ground.

We must plant our feet on firm earth —
Not on the edge of the "hole"
Of love of money or the love of women.

Lord,
Don't let us be like the pigs —
    having been cleaned up
    to return to the dirt.

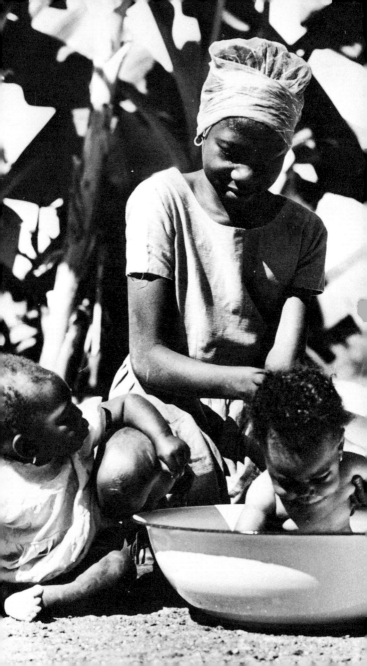

Father,
It takes a special kind of mirror
to see if our faces are dirty.
Your Word is this.

Lord,
I am a mountain farmer
   and my hand is clumsy,
      big and awkward.
I don't know how to hoe with a "sword."
      Now show me.

Lord,
Suffering is the Potter's wheel
Which turns us in the Potter's hand
    of love and affection.

Lord, take us to the creek,
   just as my wife went yesterday
      to the creek.
She took off her dress,
   beat it with a paddle,
      bathed herself in the water.
She dried her dress in the sun,
   put it on,
      and came home to me
Totally clean.

Father,
They say we are the poorest
  country in the world.
Thank You, Father.
May we also be poor in spirit,
That we may inherit the Kingdom of God.

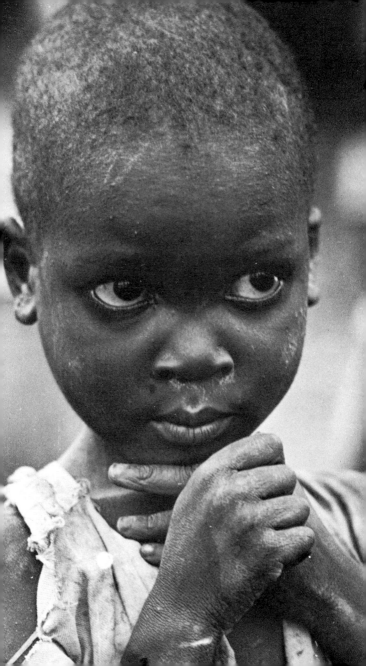

Lord,
Once I saw a woman dying, and the doctor
took the blood from Madame Wallace and
put it in the lady, and she lived.

Lord,
This morning we ask You to do
this for us — but don't let the
leeches of sin suck us dry again.

There is an angel who learned to
write without going to school.
He sits all day long writing down
all that we do.

Lord,
Help us to sow good seed,
    Since we will be the ones
        Eating from the harvest.

Lord,

There is a big devil called

      Discouragement.

We ask You to send him away because

He is bothering us.

This morning the preacher will
    distribute Your Word
Without ration cards.

Lord,
Our hearts are like a store room
For all the tools needed to do our work
Our mouths are the door to the storeroom
Now put in our hearts the tools
Of love and grace.

Lord,
What we were yesterday
Is not what we are today.
What we are today
Is not what we were yesterday.

Yesterday, we were pigs,
loving dirt and mud.
All we hated, we now love.
All we loved, we now hate.

Lord,
We stand to calculate
What we shall give the children
   to eat today,
Instead of calculating
What You have done for us.

Neighbors see us calculate,
And can't see
What You have done for us.

Lord,
Help us not to talk too much —
Because talking too much is like
    driving too fast.
Sometimes the brakes are not good,
And we pass by the place where
    we intended to stop.

When we talk too much,
We know we go beyond the truth
    and we lie.

We also know that
Speaking too much derails us from
    life's track.

Lord,
We find Your Word like a cabbage.
As we pull down the leaves,
We get closer to the heart.
And as we get closer to the heart,
It is sweeter.

Father,
A cold wind seems to have chilled us.
Wrap us in the blanket of Your Word
And warm us up a bit!

Jesus,

You are our garage.

You give us cool shade,

Make us last longer for service,

And make us beautiful.

Only then do we have value.

Lord,
May Your missionaries
Feel younger each day
To distribute Your Word.

Give them zeal
And keep them young and
unwrinkled in their souls.

Although the body may get old,
The hair white, the skin wrinkled,
Keep their souls unwrinkled.

The Mission Church at Fermathe

Wallace and Eleanor Turnbull met and married in 1948 in Haiti, where their three sons, Wally, Jr., Walter (Sandy), and David were born. They live at the mission station at Fermathe about 15 miles from the capital city, Port-au-Prince. Granny Holdeman, Mrs. Turnbull's mother, has been a co-laborer in the work since its beginning in 1947. She is known by many Child Evangelism Fellowship workers as the real-life "Granny" in the missionary adventure story entitled, *Ti-Fam: Witch Doctor's Daughter.*

Mountain View in Haiti

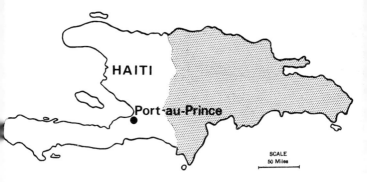

HAITI

Port-au-Prince

SCALE
50 Miles

Haiti shares with the Dominican Republic the island of Hispaniola, landing place of Columbus on his first voyage to the new world. France replaced Spanish control in 1697, imported slaves from Africa, and turned the tropical island into a vast estate of sugar, coffee and cotton plantations. During the French Revolution Haiti defeated Napoleon's troops and declared her independence in 1804.

In addition to many political difficulties, this mountainous country of 5,000,000 people has staggering spiritual and economic problems. Voodooism, the people's religion in Haiti, originated in Africa. It is a form of ancestor worship in which witch doctors use weird fetishes and ceremonies to keep the people in constant fear of attack by the dead and evil spirits because of imagined slight or neglect. Haiti has also been ravaged by droughts and hurricanes in recent years, causing chronic hunger and starvation.

The Conservative Baptist Haiti Mission Society, Inc.
An independent, evangelical Baptist Mission serving Christ in Haiti

- 58 national churches, 47 outstations, serving 30,000 Haitians

- Mission hospital and four dispensaries supervised by two Haitian doctors, staffed by national personnel, and serving 14,000 patients yearly

- 87 literacy schools for 5,400 mountain children

- Three-month summer Bible institute for 100 church leaders

- Youth and adult Bible conferences

- Revolving loan fund to help erect church buildings

- Extensive relief and reconstruction program for hurricane and drought

- Community development after storms — road construction, soil conservation terracing program

- Agriculture Improvement Program in fertilizer, seeds and animal husbandry

The mission is supported by the free-will offering of individuals and churches. You are invited to invest in this needy field which has one of the fastest growing Christian communities, mostly first-generation converts from Voodooism. All contributions are tax-exempt and will be acknowledged by letter and receipt. For additional information you may write to:

The Conservative Baptist Haiti Mission
1537 N. Plainfield Ave.
Grand Rapids, Michigan 49505